# LIVING IN NORTH KOREA

John Allen

ReferencePoint
Press

San Diego, CA

About the Author

John Allen is a writer who lives in Oklahoma City.

© 2019 ReferencePoint Press, Inc.
Printed in the United States

**For more information, contact:**
ReferencePoint Press, Inc.
PO Box 27779
San Diego, CA 92198
www.ReferencePointPress.com

Picture Credits:

Cover: Kyodo/Associated Press
 4: Maury Aaseng (map); G7 Stock/Shutterstock.com (flag)
 5: Viktoria Gaman/Shutterstock.com (first and second images); Asia Images/Shutterstock.com (third image); iStockphoto.com (bottom image)
 9: LMspencer/Shutterstock.com
12: Richard Bradford/Shutterstock.com
15: Associated Press
19: Associated Press
22: Associated Press
30: Associated Press
33: Associated Press
37: Associated Press
43: alexkuehni/iStockphoto.com
46: Associated Press
49: Kyodo/Newscom
53: Freda Bouskoutas/iStockphoto.com
57: Freda Bouskoutas/iStockphoto.com
63: Associated Press
65: Kyodo/Newscom
69: iStockphoto.com

LIBRARY OF CONGRESS CATALOGING-IN-PUBLICATION DATA

Name: Allen, John, 1957– author.
Title: Living in North Korea/by John Allen.
Description: San Diego, CA: ReferencePoint Press, Inc., [2019] | Includes bibliographical references and index. | Audience: Grades 9–12.
Identifiers: LCCN 2018025986 (print) | LCCN 2018027972 (ebook) | ISBN 9781682824764 (eBook) | ISBN 9781682824757 (hardback)
Subjects: LCSH: Korea (North)—Social conditions—21st century—Juvenile literature. | Korea (North)—Social life and customs—21st century—Juvenile literature. | Korea (North)—Politics and government—2011—Juvenile literature.
Classification: LCC HN730.6.A8 (ebook) | LCC HN730.6.A8 A44 2019 (print) | DDC 306.095193—dc23
LC record available at https://lccn.loc.gov/2018025986

# CONTENTS

# NORTH KOREA AT A GLANCE

**Official Name**
Democratic People's
Republic of Korea

**Size**
46,541 square miles
(120,541 sq. km)

**Total Population**
25,248,140 as of 2017

**Youth Population**
0–14 years: 20.78%;
15–24 years: 15.59%

**Capital**
Pyongyang

**Type of Government**
Single-party state with
official ideology of *juche*,
or "national self-reliance"

**Language**
Korean

**Currency**
North Korean *won*

**Industries**
Military products; machine building;
electric power; chemicals; mining
(coal, iron ore, limestone, magnesite,
graphite, copper, zinc, lead, and
precious metals); metallurgy; textiles;
food processing; tourism

**Literacy**
100% (age 15+ able
to read and write)

**Internet Users**
Limited to a small number of
elite users and scientists

# INTRODUCTION

## The Hermit Kingdom

Some North Koreans will do almost anything to escape their nation's prison-like borders. At age seventeen, Hyeonseo Lee fled on foot across the frozen Yalu River into neighboring China in quest of a better life. She survived frightening encounters with gangsters, pimps, and Chinese police before finally reaching South Korea and asylum. Having established a home in Seoul, Lee returned to China to help smuggle her mother and brother out of North Korea. She later wrote a book about her homeland and her experiences as a refugee. Her podcasts about North Korea caused a worldwide sensation on the Internet for their candid portrait of her home country. Today it is defectors, or political refugees, like Lee who provide the most reliable information about daily life in North Korea. Lee despises the repressive government in her native land, and she holds nothing back in describing the terrible conditions the people face. However, she also can evoke the simple pleasures of family life there. "Every word I'm speaking, it's not from myself," she says. "I'm speaking for and representing the people of communist North Korea."[1]

### A Paranoid Desire for Control

With its zeal for secrecy and seclusion, North Korea has long been called the Hermit Kingdom. It separated from South Korea after a Communist revolt in the late 1940s. Since then the nation has followed a path of totalitarian control. Kim Jong Un, North Korea's supreme leader, displays a paranoid desire to stifle outside influences and control every aspect of citizens' lives. From birth, the nation's 25 million people are fed a steady diet of propaganda about the near godlike qualities of Kim and his forebears.

The government controls all news and information. Through the state-run media, North Koreans are told of their country's matchless standard of living. Stories about poverty, famine, and prison camps do not appear in state media. In fact, among 197 nations ranked for press freedom by the research group Freedom House, North Korea ranks dead last.

Information sources, from newspapers to television shows, must slavishly follow the government line. Radios are wired so as to pick up only government frequencies. Even the Internet operates under strict control by the state. Citizens with computers and cell phones are restricted to a state-run system with a limited number of websites. Government officials with special privileges can access the wider Internet, but even they are blocked from many sites. As a result, North Koreans tend to have limited knowledge of the outside world.

Movement inside the country also is tightly controlled. The average family cannot simply pack up and move to another part of the country in search of better jobs or schools. A special permit is required to travel from one province to another. The capital of Pyongyang, where most high-profile jobs are located, is generally closed to those who do not live there. Although internal travel is rare, hundreds of thousands of North Koreans have been relocated by force to less desirable areas as punishment for political offenses.

In the countryside, life is marked by hard work and little reward. People grow accustomed to a narrow world made up of family members, neighbors, and a few acquaintances. Shortages of food and household items are taken for granted. Bans on eating meat, which is scarce throughout the country, lead some to inform on neighbors who obtain meat via illegal vendors. Many citizens suspect the government is lying to them. But they refrain from speaking out for fear of winding up in a prison camp. People try to make the best of things, even as government intimidation rules their lives. "The level of fear is unimaginable," says Korean American journalist Suki Kim, who once taught English to elites in North Korea. "It's possible to be both happy and terrified all at once, and I think that's the case for many North Koreans."[2]

## Rising Tensions

Kim Jong Un's distrust of the United States has led to rising tensions between the two countries. Like his father, Kim Jong Il, the younger Kim has been focused on developing nuclear weapons. North Korea has tested long-range missiles capable of striking far beyond the Korean Peninsula. Nuclear experts agree they now can reach anywhere on the American mainland, including Washington, DC, although that is without the weight of a nuclear warhead. Kim has exchanged threats with President Donald Trump, who early in his presidency dismissed the dictator as "Little Rocket Man."[3] Kim's propaganda factory paints the United States as a failing country out to destroy North Korea. Many North Koreans assume this is true, although they also enjoy smuggled films and TV shows from America.

> "The level of fear is unimaginable. It's possible to be both happy and terrified all at once, and I think that's the case for many North Koreans."[2]
>
> —Suki Kim, a Korean American journalist who once taught English in North Korea

Just as the government strives to keep its people in the dark, it works hard to keep facts about North Korea from reaching the outside world. Foreign journalists are not allowed to wander about the country on their own. Instead, they are escorted to carefully chosen sites. Tourists must stay with guides, who monitor every step they take. Government officials deflect probing questions or cut interviews short if they stray into unwanted areas. At the 2018 Winter Olympics in Pyeongchang, South Korea, two hundred red-clad young women from North Korea drew a great deal of attention worldwide for their choreographed cheers. Yet none were allowed to speak to the foreign press. When outside news agencies report on North Korea, they are limited in what they can show. Most reports include shots of gleaming skyscrapers and stock footage of military parades overseen by a smiling Kim. The impoverished lives of rural North Koreans are never seen.

Statues of North Korea's former leaders tower over residents in the capital city of Pyongyang. Idealized images of the country's former leaders (the father and grandfather of current leader Kim Jong Un) can be seen throughout North Korea.

With this information blockade in place, the world relies on reports from academics who study North Korea, journalists who document aspects of North Korean life despite the obstacles, and the occasional humanitarian aid organization that has permission to provide services in the country. However, the most revealing information comes from defectors like Hyeonseo Lee. Many of these refugees have risked their lives to escape North Korea. They consider it their mission to provide the truth about their homeland. "North Korea is not the dictator's country," says Lee. "It's 25 million citizens' country, and they are suffering under the dictator. North Koreans are really nice, kind, pure people. I hate the dictator and the regime, but I love my home country."[4]

> "North Korea is not the dictator's country, it's 25 million citizens' country, and they are suffering under the dictator."[4]
>
> —Hyeonseo Lee, a defector from North Korea

# CHAPTER ONE

# A Nation Under Rigid Control

The Democratic People's Republic of Korea, or North Korea, lies south of China and Russia on the northern end of the Korean Peninsula. The peninsula is divided roughly in half between North Korea and South Korea. The two nations share a border along the 38th parallel. A strip of land called the Korean Demilitarized Zone (DMZ) serves as a buffer between the two countries. The DMZ, established in the 1953 settlement of the Korean War, is 160 miles (257 km) long and 2.5 miles (4 km) wide. Both North Korea and South Korea still claim rights to the entire peninsula, but the two have existed in an uneasy truce for decades. Relatively few outsiders have visited North Korea during this period. Its government rules by force and fear, preserving its isolation from the world.

## Crisscrossed by Mountains

The difficulty of life in North Korea contrasts with the beauty of the country's forested landscape. More than 80 percent of North Korea's 46,541 square miles (120,541 sq. km) is crisscrossed by mountain ranges divided by deep, narrow valleys. Forests, most of them on steep slopes, occupy 70 percent of the land. In the northeast, the Kaema Highlands rise more than 3,300 feet (1,006 m) above sea level. Among the Changbai Mountains at the northern end of this plateau sits Mount Paektu, the tallest mountain on the Korean Peninsula. This legendary 9,000-foot (2,743 m) peak is an active volcano capped by a large crater lake. The Nangnim Mountains extend through the middle of the country, separating the eastern and western slopes. In the east are areas of flatlands. Along the east coast, the Taebaek Mountains run from southern

North Korea into South Korea. Mount Kumgang in the far southeast is known for the beauty of its forests, cliffs, and spectacular waterfalls.

Water resources in North Korea include a large network of rivers that drain into the Yellow Sea. The Yellow Sea and Korea Bay lie to the west, with Japan located to the east across the Sea of Japan. North Korea's longest river is the Yalu. From the southern slope of Mount Paektu, the Yalu flows southwest to its mouth on Korea Bay, a distance of about 500 miles (805 km). Like the Yalu, the largest rivers drain to the Yellow Sea in the west. The wide plains and valleys along these rivers feature rich soil for agriculture. Elsewhere, the soils are mostly ash-gray forest mixtures, as in the highlands, or sandy and poor for growing.

North Korea has a relatively cool continental climate overall. Winters generally are clear and cold, with occasional snowstorms barreling in from Siberia. Summers are warm and humid, marked by frequent heavy rains of the Pacific monsoon. Sixty percent of annual precipitation falls from June to September. Flooding in the north can sometimes be disastrous. In September 2016 torrential rains from Typhoon Lionrock caused many levees to fail, leading to floods in one of the nation's poorest regions. Rising floodwaters wiped out entire villages. Tens of thousands lost their homes. Shortly after the typhoon hit, Darlene Tymo, of the United Nations World Food Programme, stated, "Families have lost everything, including their kitchen gardens and livestock, which many households depend upon to supplement their diets."[5]

North Korea features a wealth of plants and wildlife, but today the landscape is changing. On the highlands around Mount Paektu are found trees such as spruce, pine, Siberian fir, and Korean pine. The western plains, once a rich ground for mixed forests and plants, have been overcut until only patches of the original forests remain. The lowlands are mostly cultivated, with surrounding hills covered with pine groves, oaks, maples, and birches. Rural streams are good sources for river fish such as eels and carp, but deforestation has reduced the habitat for many

The Mount Paektu volcano (foreground) is the tallest mountain on the Korean Peninsula. It is distinguished by a huge crater lake at its summit and by its sacred place in Korean history.

forms of wildlife, such as antelope, deer, tigers, and leopards. The plains still host large numbers of herons, cranes, and wild pigeons, which linger in the rice fields. Oddly enough, the DMZ has become one of the most unspoiled areas for plants and wildlife in all of Asia. Without human occupation, it provides sanctuary to hundreds of species of birds and fish. Mammals such as Asiatic black bears and lynxes also thrive there.

## Famine and Low Population Growth

Reliable data about North Korea's population is hard to find. The last national census was completed in 2008 and its findings released in 2011. Due to North Korea's policy of isolation, its population is anything but diverse. The great majority of its 25 million people are ethnically Korean, with only a few pockets of Chinese, Vietnamese, and ethnic Japanese. About 36 percent are age twenty-four or younger. Most of the population lives in the plains and lowlands in the southern and western parts of the country.

The mountainous regions in the north contain few people. Sixty percent of North Korea's people live in urban areas. The largest city is the capital, Pyongyang, with a population of 3.2 million. It is the nation's only city with more than 1 million residents. Vast areas of the countryside remain sparsely settled and completely undeveloped. Because of persistent food shortages and lack of housing space, the population struggles to grow at 1 percent per year.

Famine has played a large part in limiting growth. For example, in 1995 severe floods from a warm El Niño weather pattern wrecked 15 percent of the nation's farmland. This flooding, followed by a long period of drought, triggered a four-year famine. The government's push for collective farming had already served to disrupt food production. The Soviet Union's collapse brought

## Claiming the Legacy of Mount Paektu

Mount Paektu, the towering volcano that lies along North Korea's border with China, forms a vital part of the nation's mythology. Legends describe how the first Korean people descended from this majestic peak. In 946 it produced one of the largest volcanic eruptions in history. It is pictured in North Korea's national emblem, as well as in countless paintings, drawings, and photographs. Its name appears on everything from rockets to power stations. Having last erupted in 1903, Mount Paektu is viewed today as a scenic wonder, with silvery clouds reflected in the calm blue waters of its crater lake.

But like everything else in the nation, Mount Paektu has been transformed by the Kim dynasty into a symbol of the family's exalted station. North Korean schoolchildren learn about how Kim Il Sung and his guerrilla fighters launched attacks against the occupying Japanese from the slopes of Mount Paektu. His son, Kim Jong Il, claimed a wooden cabin on Mount Paektu as his own birthplace, although he was actually born in a Russian refugee camp. By way of the *juche* ideology, the Kims have promoted themselves as the divine Mount Paektu bloodline. The Korean people are programmed to link the Kims with their nation's sacred mountain. In April 2015 Kim Jong Il's son, Kim Jong Un, posed for photographs at the summit of Mount Paektu. The state news agency reported, in one of its typical falsehoods, that the young ruler had climbed to the top himself.

an end to food subsidies from Russia, and China also reduced its aid. North Korean officials reacted by seizing stored grain from farm families. Desperate for food, citizens in rural areas tried to live off the land. In some areas frogs were hunted until they were almost extinct. Jobless and weak from hunger, workers roamed the streets of major cities. "The government started a campaign urging citizens to consume less," says Jordan Weissmann, a foreign affairs writer for the *Atlantic*. "Its cheery slogan: 'Let's eat only two meals a day.'"[6] Starvation, along with illnesses related to lack of food, led to the deaths of 2 million to 3 million North Koreans.

North Korea's economy operates under the smothering control of the government. The regime has failed to make substantial improvements in the people's standard of living. For example, many midlevel workers still subsist on a meatless diet and wear cheap clothes and plastic shoes. The government claims that its distribution system provides for all the people's needs, but many rural citizens lack access to food rations and other necessities. In 2015 the average North Korean made the equivalent of about $30 to $40 a month. In contrast, the average South Korean made more than $2,000 a month. North Korea's economy lags far behind the market-based economy of South Korea. In 2013 (the most recent year for which statistics are available), North Korea's gross domestic product was $33 billion, while South Korea's was $1.19 trillion. Lack of food and resources has had a physical effect on many in the North. According to Daniel Schwekendiek, a professor in Seoul, North Koreans on average are about two inches shorter than their counterparts in South Korea.

The North's main industries are machine building, mining, metallurgy, textiles, and food processing. Although its economy struggles, North Korea has the potential for fabulous wealth. Experts believe the country holds vast deposits of minerals valued at from $6 trillion to $10 trillion. Lack of suitable mining

Textile factory workers are busy at their sewing machines in the northeastern corner of the country. Textiles are one of North Korea's primary industries.

equipment and technology makes it difficult for North Korea to harvest this wealth on its own. Ultimately, it must look to China and Russia for help in developing this stockpile of minerals.

## A Communist Takeover

North Korea depended on the influence of China and Russia from its beginning. It was founded as a Communist state in 1948, organized on the model of Soviet Russia. Its revolutionary project, based on the Socialist ideas of Karl Marx and Vladimir Lenin, sought to end ownership of property and mistreatment of workers. In practice, however, the government became an iron-fisted dictatorship, which it remains to this day.

From 1910 to 1945 Japan ruled the entire Korean Peninsula. The Japanese exploited the Korean people, sowing bitterness that lasts today. After Japan's defeat in World War II, the Allies divided the peninsula at the 38th parallel. By agreement, the Soviets took control of the northern half, helping create a Soviet-style Communist state. The United States and its Western allies administered the southern half, which became the Republic of Korea.

Kim Il Sung, a longtime Korean revolutionary and guerrilla fighter, crushed all rivals to become sole leader of North Korea. Kim admired Soviet ruler Joseph Stalin, and he followed Stalin's example by placing every part of society under government control. A single political party, the Workers' Party of Korea, held all power. Kim served as party chair. "Kim Il Sung masterminded a unique adaptation of Soviet totalitarianism so that North Korea turned out to be more Stalinist than Stalin himself," says historian Lucian W. Pye. "Indeed, Kim's commitment to [Communist ideas of] Marxism-Leninism was stronger than that of the Soviet bloc regimes in Eastern Europe or the communist regimes of China and Vietnam."[7] Under Kim, the North Korean government seized land from rich families and redistributed it to peasant farmers. The state also took control of many private industries, introduced labor laws to protect workers, and gave women new rights. Citizens who opposed the new regime soon found themselves in prison or facing a firing squad.

> "Kim Il Sung masterminded a unique adaptation of Soviet totalitarianism so that North Korea turned out to be more Stalinist than Stalin himself."[7]
>
> —Historian Lucian W. Pye

Attempts to unify the two parts of Korea through the United Nations went nowhere. In 1950 war broke out between North and South Korea. Armed with Soviet tanks, artillery, and rifles, the North Korean army invaded the South in an attempt to unify the peninsula under a Communist government. The bloody civil war continued for three years, with the Soviet Union and China backing the North and joint United Nations forces, including US troops, aiding the South. US bombing raids in the North left hundreds of thousands dead and prompted among North Koreans a longstanding bitterness toward America. The conflict ended in a cease-fire but no peace treaty, a situation that lasts to this day.

## Of Firing Squads and Assassinations

As many defectors have affirmed, public executions are commonplace in today's North Korea. They serve as bloody warnings that rebellion against Kim Jong Un's brutal regime will not be tolerated. People can be executed for crimes such as stealing grain or livestock or distributing media materials from South Korea. Executions often take place outside prison walls—in riverbeds, beside bridges, in sports stadiums, and in local market squares. Some prisoners have been executed by firing squads on school grounds, with pupils required to attend. These public killings, carried out before large crowds, serve to create an atmosphere of dread in the populace.

Fiendish methods of execution are reserved for those deemed to be dangerous enemies of the regime. In February 2017 Kim was enraged by five government officials who supposedly spread false reports about North Korea. Kim sentenced them to face a bizarre firing squad consisting of an antiaircraft gun—thus blowing the accused officials to bits. Kim has also been resourceful in dealing with family members he considers a threat. In a Malaysian airport on February 13, 2017, two young women, one wearing a T-shirt that said LOL, smeared poisonous chemicals on the face of Kim's estranged elder brother, Kim Jong Nam. Within minutes Kim Jong Nam lay dead in the airport clinic. His crime was telling a Japanese journalist that his brother was "a joke to the outside world" and predicting that his brother's regime would not last long.

Quoted in Doug Bock Clark, "The Untold Story of Kim Jong-nam's Assassination," *GQ*, September 25, 2017. www.gq.com.

## A Move Toward Self-Reliance

After the war, Kim consolidated his grip on the country. Although the Supreme People's Assembly held votes for president, in reality Kim made himself ruler for life. All who opposed him were tried and executed or driven out of government, leaving only those who never raised objections to his whims. He ruled with casual cruelty, ordering farmers whipped for hoarding grain or jailing workers for wrapping food in newspapers bearing his picture. Kim created a cult of personality, in which North Koreans considered him to be inseparable from the state. Some in the North came to obsess over

Kim's superhuman qualities. "I had to be careful of my thoughts," recalls Park Yeon-mi, a North Korean defector and human rights activist, "because I believed Kim Jong-il could read my mind."[8]

Over the years, Kim replaced the country's Communist ideology with a more nationalist doctrine called *juche*. The word roughly translates to "self-reliance." It began as a political catch-phrase in the 1950s, when word of Stalin's crimes in Russia was causing support for Communist ideals to ebb. The Workers' Party used the juche philosophy to inspire people in the face of worsening conditions and shrinking support from the Soviet Union. The forced self-reliance of juche served to emphasize the isolation of the Hermit Kingdom. Juche came to influence every part of North Korean society. While still Socialist in theory, it advanced the idea that each North Korean is in control of his or her own destiny. It declared that through strength and personal will, the nation's people could achieve great things, including true socialism. Juche also evolved to include principles of self-defense, sustainable agriculture, and economic independence. It developed into a virtual state religion in an antireligious nation. "Juche serves as an ideological tool for unifying the country," says Donald Baker, professor of Korean history at the University of British Columbia. "It says, 'We don't need God. Instead, we rely on the leader.'"[9]

> "Juche serves as an ideological tool for unifying the country. It says, 'We don't need God. Instead, we rely on the leader.'"[9]
>
> —Donald Baker, professor of Korean history at the University of British Columbia

Kim used juche to promote the idea that he and his children were virtually divine beings. He claimed to have been born in a secret military camp on Mount Paektu, the mythical birthplace of the Korean people. More than forty thousand statues and monuments around the country celebrate his godlike status. When Kim Il Sung died in 1994, leadership passed to his son, Kim Jong Il. The son ruled until his own death in 2011. Today Kim Jong Un, the grandson of Kim Il Sung and third in the so-called Paektu bloodline, holds the reins of power as the person North Koreans refer to as "Dear Leader."[10]

## Military First

Kim Jong Un was not yet thirty years old when his father died. Despite having been groomed for leadership, he has little experience in economics or diplomacy. Kim has done more to stifle the people's freedom and alarm the world with nuclear threats than grow the economy or improve conditions of daily life. Like his father and grandfather, Kim diverts the nation's resources into the military—a policy known as *songun*, or "military first." Of the nation's 25 million people, 1 million are soldiers. The government spends more than one-fifth of the nation's gross domestic product on the military; frequent power blackouts and severe

North Korean soldiers march in a military parade in 2017. The country's leader prizes military might and prestige over all other needs.

food shortages get much less attention and money. The lure of military might and prestige outweighs all other considerations. In 2016, when the United States led efforts to impose sanctions on North Korea for its nuclear tests, Kim made it clear that his nation would not be deterred from developing nuclear weapons. "When they tighten their belts," says John Delury, an assistant professor at Yonsei University in Seoul, "the last thing they cut is the military."[11]

Recently, Kim suspended nuclear tests ahead of the June 2018 meeting with President Donald Trump. He announced at a major party gathering that the government would focus more on shoring up the economy. State media showered praise on Kim for his wisdom in dealing with the nation's enemies.

The historic June 12 meeting between Kim and Trump also brought lavish praise from North Korea's media—although ordinary citizens heard nothing about the meeting's outcome until the day after it took place. State media applauded Kim's achievements, saying his earlier actions and his performance at the summit are leading to a new era of peace and prosperity. Although Kim and Trump issued a joint statement after the meeting, it was short on specifics. Nevertheless, complimentary coverage of the country's leader is standard fare in North Korea.

What average North Koreans did not see were any of the stories filed by media from other countries, some of which recognized the history-making moment but questioned whether there would be an equally historic long-term outcome. These and other sentiments are not likely to be heard or read inside North Korea. For now, the regime's system of rigid control shows no signs of relenting. Despite its natural beauty and resilient people, North Korea remains an isolated and impoverished nation.

# CHAPTER TWO

## Family Life

Daily life for most families in North Korea tends to follow traditional patterns that go back decades, if not centuries. Visitors rarely glimpse the living conditions of ordinary North Koreans. Families in small cities and rural villages struggle to get by, while those in the capital city of Pyongyang often enjoy more privileges. The government claims its citizens are thriving, but it seems bent on keeping out any prying eyes. "Trying to find out what life is like in North Korea is a bit like trying to find out if the light turns off when you close the fridge door," says Michael Turtle, a journalist who traveled to North Korea several years ago. "You can never truly look inside and discover anything with certainty, but by talking with people and keeping your eyes open, you can start to get a basic sense of things."[12]

### Social Status for Newborns

At birth a child enters the North Korean government system. All parents must register the birth of a baby. Information on the new citizen is stored in three locations: the local town hall, the local police station, and headquarters of the state-run secret police. The state also registers the newborn's *songbun*, or social status. (The word *songbun* means "background" in Korean.) This determines much about the path in life for new citizens, including where they will live and work, which university they can attend, and whether they can join the military or the Korean Workers' Party. An army of bureaucrats works overtime to create and maintain detailed records for songbun. The regime uses a special software, called Faithful Servant 2.0, to run the songbun system.

   A police officer stamps the baby's new file—which is actually part of the parents' file until age seventeen—with one of three broad songbun classifications. These are based on the status of the infant's father. The categories include Core, Wavering, and Hostile. Children marked Core receive the best the state has to offer. Those labeled Hostile may be treated almost as enemies of the state, with few handouts and a constant threat of exile or prison camp. In theory, the state provides everything a citizen needs for life through the Public Distribution System. Since the 1990s, however, this system has mostly broken down due to shortages and economic troubles. Only elite families can count on steady support.

The songbun system can place hard limits on human potential. For example, Choi Seung Chol, born in 1990, faced hardships from an early age due to his grandfather's actions. The state designated Choi's grandfather as a supporter of the hated Japanese in World War II. As a result, the family was forced to move from its city home to a mountain village in the eastern part of the country.

A nurse comforts a baby at a nursery inside a Pyongyang maternity hospital. At birth, a baby's name and official social classification are registered with the government.

Choi's grandfather, father, and other relatives worked long hours in the fields for decades before authorities finally allowed the family to move back to a coastal city.

Although Choi was a gifted student, his prospects were limited. He tried everything to overcome the cloud over his family's name. He woke early to clean shrines to North Korean leaders to show party loyalty. He became head of the youth league at his school. His parents even paid bribes to party officials to boost his chances of advancement. In the end none of it mattered. The supposed crime of the grandfather continued to stain the grandson. All Choi's applications to the top universities were rejected. Hopes of joining the military or becoming a high-ranking official in Pyongyang were soon dashed. Like others crushed in the songbun system, Choi felt helpless. In 2014 he escaped to South Korea in search of a better life. "Unless you have a way to the top," says Choi, "there is no hope, nothing left but hard work with no return and constant fear and payment of bribes to be able to barely go out. That is why I decided to leave."[13]

## Family Size and Structure

Whether living in urban or rural areas, families in North Korea tend to be small. A typical family consists of four or five people under one roof. Unlike the traditional arrangement of the past, it is rare today for more than two generations to live together. Older parents of limited means may live with their youngest son and his wife. Large extended families living together has become quite unusual. Sons are considered more desirable than daughters, mainly to carry on the family name.

In 2015 Radio Free Asia reported that the North Korean government had set up new rules forbidding doctors to implant birth control devices or perform abortions. The rules were intended to reverse the nation's falling birthrate. Refugees say that abortions can still be obtained in cities, though the procedure is very expensive and doctors face a large fine if discovered. Often, an abortion is performed in a doctor's home, not only to preserve secrecy but to avoid unsanitary conditions in state hospitals. According to Je Son Lee, who recently left North Korea:

> In the past, if people were friends with an obstetrician, they would bring liquor and cigarettes and ask them to perform the operation as a favor. . . . Because of the dangers, people began to avoid having abortions performed by obstetricians at the hospital, and many doctors began to perform abortions in more hygienic conditions and in the possession of proper medical equipment at their homes.[14]

Families in which both spouses work often place their infants in a *t'agaso*, or day care nursery, until age four. State-run nurseries, like the one attached to the Changchon vegetable farm outside Pyongyang, mix day care with propaganda. Toddlers at the Changchon nursery watch hours of *Squirrel and Hedgehog*, an animated show featuring the residents of Flower Hill. The animals include squirrels as military leaders, hedgehogs as soldiers, and ducks as sailors. "As you might guess, this squadron represents North Korea," says Julie Makinen, a journalist for the *Los Angeles Times*. "The Flower Hill gang must contend with evil weasels (Japan) and wolves (the United States), while occasionally dealing with friendly but drunk bears (Russia)."[15]

"Because of the dangers, people began to avoid having abortions performed by obstetricians at the hospital, and many doctors began to perform abortions in more hygienic conditions and in the possession of proper medical equipment at their homes."[14]

—Je Son Lee, a recent defector from North Korea

In recent years Kim Jong Un has ordered a crackdown on private day care centers and preschools. The official reason given for the crackdown was to standardize the care and teaching of young children. But, according to sources at Radio Free Asia, Kim's real goal is to eliminate any threat to state control of education and propaganda. Anyone operating an illegal day care facility faces exile to a rural area. As a result, working couples must

## Origins of Songbun

The Korean Workers' Party created the songbun classification system in 1957. The idea was to protect Kim Il Sung's regime by weeding out those who were disloyal. Every citizen was assigned a loyalty class based on family background. The three classes—Core, Wavering, and Hostile—basically boil down to friendly, neutral, and enemy classifications. The system eventually came to include about fifty-one subgroupings. These cover almost every imaginable instance of background and behavior, from heroic loyalty to traitorous opposition.

Today the Core category includes about 28 percent of the population. Those considered Core citizens come from families who fought to liberate Korea from the Japanese in 1945. Their forebears may also have been peasants or full-time revolutionaries—both categories favored by Kim's Marxist leanings. The Wavering class consists of nearly 45 percent of the people. These citizens remain under suspicion because family members once lived in China or South Korea or included small merchants or intellectuals. The Hostile group includes about 27 percent of the population. These are descendants of capitalists, landlords, religious believers, and those who helped South Korean troops during the Korean War. They are judged to be enemies of the party and possibly traitors. The slightest misstep can land a citizen classed as Hostile in a prison camp or in front of a firing squad. According to Sokeel J. Park, a South Korean policy analyst, "The implementation of songbun therefore creates considerable fear and forces people to obey the regime."

Sokeel J. Park, "Songbun: Social Class in a Socialist Paradise," *Liberty in North Korea* (blog), June 25, 2012. www.libertyinnorthkorea.org.

scramble to find alternatives. Some leave infants with grandparents for the day. In other families the husband will stay home with young children while the wife goes to work in a factory.

## High-Rises and Concrete Houses

Housing varies a great deal between urban and rural areas. In Pyongyang and other large cities, families tend to live in enormous high-rise buildings, from ten to forty stories in height. Residential neighborhoods feature row upon row of identical buildings. The high-rises are surrounded by wide boulevards, monuments, and large open squares where children like to go rollerblading. Families on upper floors often face problems due to a shortage of electricity. When the power is out, as happens all too often with North Korea's unreliable electric grid, elevators do not operate, and climbing stairs is the only option. For this reason, upper-level apartments are traded at a discount. Some elderly residents on upper floors have not left their buildings in years.

Apartments are small with few frills. In theory, the state provides furnishings, so most families own only a few pieces of furniture and household goods. On the walls of every home are portraits of Kim Jong Un and his father or grandfather. Appliances

## Travel Restrictions in North Korea

North Koreans have few options regarding travel. They face severe restrictions on traveling outside the country. As business reporter Charles Clark notes, "If you're born in North Korea, you'll probably never be allowed to leave North Korea." Under Kim Jong Un's rule, no one can leave the nation without permission from the state. North Korean passports are temporary and issued only to high-ranking officials. They are used for limited business or diplomatic travel or for visits to relatives in China. A North Korean passport is one of the most restrictive in the world, granting access to only forty-one countries.

Families or individuals who seek to travel inside North Korea to another province or city are also stymied. The government maintains military checkpoints throughout the country to prevent freedom of movement. Few people are seen on rural roads. Permission to travel must come from the citizen's work unit. A person must offer a specific purpose for traveling. Relocating to get a better job is not an option. Those living outside the privileged districts of Pyongyang likely have no chance to obtain a travel pass. Nonetheless, should the regime choose, a family can be relocated without notice to a faraway province as political punishment.

Charles Clark, "Here's What It's Like Inside a North Korean Passport—One of the World's Rarest Travel Documents," Business Insider, September 15, 2016. www.businessinsider.com.

are becoming more commonplace, although problems with intermittent power make them less useful. Central heating rarely functions. In the winter many apartment dwellers build small fires for warmth, despite dangers from inhaling smoke.

Private ownership of homes is illegal in North Korea. Nonetheless, a black market has emerged for apartments in Pyongyang and along the border with China. Homes close to China are prized for better Internet connections and access to Chinese commerce. Families that have accumulated hard currency can pay bribes to public officials to obtain larger apartments in better neighborhoods. The best apartments are reserved for party members with special privileges. Due to songbun and government control, ordinary workers have few options if they want a better home in a more desirable district.

Forty percent of North Korea's families live in the countryside. Rural villages in North Korea consist of simple houses of concrete built close together. Villagers travel back and forth by bicycle on dirt roads. Many houses look like they are still under construction, with partial fences and buckling roofs. A few towns feature newer homes the government built after floods ravaged the area. Power failures are frequent, although the power grid is improving. Some towns have turned to solar panels to supply electricity. A few family dwellings have mini generators imported from China to power televisions and lamps. Rural homes often rely on wood fires for cooking and heat. Many lack running water and flush toilets.

## Importance of Meals

In cities or the countryside, daily meals are important gatherings for the typical family. Parents and children gather at mealtime in the evening to eat and discuss the events of the day. By necessity, most families make do with small amounts of protein. Instead, they rely on boiled rice and porridge. Even kimchi, the traditional Korean dish made of fermented cabbage, cucumbers, and fiery red chilies, has become a rarity.

At each meal, the oldest person raises a chopstick or spoon to begin. Children are taught to say *jalmukesumneda*, which means "I will eat well." Breakfast consists of porridge made from corn and soybeans that are mashed and cooked to create a spicy sausage. There might also be a boiled egg and sour yogurt, with powdered milk for the children. At dinner, family members sit around a low table set with several bowls of food. The bowls contain rice and perhaps a few vegetable dumplings fried in oil. With sugar in short supply, sweets are a rare treat for children. Sometimes a family may obtain *kongsatang*, or bean candy, from a street seller. This is made from roasted soybeans coated with sugar or glucose made from grapes. Despite a shortage of nutritious food, family members make the best of things. Mealtimes are full of storytelling and cheerful banter. The table becomes a jumble of arms and chopsticks as everyone reaches for the different bowls.

## Meager Diets

Although the government insists food supplies are improving, 10.3 million North Koreans remain undernourished. According to international aid officials, the food situation for families is dire. A severe drought in 2015 reduced harvests by 11 percent and worsened the food shortage. As the World Food Programme reports:

> Many people suffer from chronic malnutrition due to lack of essential proteins, fats, vitamins and minerals. Those living in towns and cities have worse diets, with many relying on rural relatives, improvised "kitchen gardens" or market activities to supplement the food they receive through the Government's Public Distribution System (PDS). The PDS consistently provides lower food rations than the Government's daily target.[16]

Families that buy extra food do not go to a grocery store. Many procure dishes from street vendors or illegal markets. The latter are also called grasshopper markets, because of the speed at which the stalls are set up and then whisked away to escape police. These street hawkers sell a variety of makeshift low-calorie, low-protein items. *Injogogibab*, nicknamed man-made meat, is made from soybean oil. The oil is pressed and rolled into a hard paste, dried to a tortilla-like texture, then topped with chili sauce. Tofu and other forms of vegetable protein also are available. These meat substitutes, which were introduced to help families survive the famines of the 1990s, serve to supplement the national diet.

> "Many people suffer from chronic malnutrition due to lack of essential proteins, fats, vitamins and minerals."[16]
>
> —World Food Programme report on North Korea

Many North Koreans think of real meat as a holiday extravagance or an unaffordable delicacy. Kim Jong Un's government has urged families to eat *dangogi*, or dog meat, touting it as a so-called superfood rich in vitamins. Dog carcasses often are hung in street markets alongside the occasional duck or chicken.

## Lifestyle of Privileged Families

In Pyongyang, families with ties to the upper levels of the party or military enjoy a lifestyle their fellow citizens can only dream about. Under the songbun system, their political loyalty and family history ensure that they are insulated from food shortages and economic troubles. These families have cars, relatively spacious homes, reliable electricity, smartphones, video games and electronics, and some access to the wider Internet. Their children know the latest songs and dance moves from South Korea's K-pop culture. Children and young adults who are not painfully thin like so many North Koreans probably belong to privileged families with plenty to eat.

The most elite families—including those of military officers, top bureaucrats, party officials, diplomats, and business leaders—receive endless benefits from the regime. They vacation at an east coast beach resort in the summer and travel to a luxurious ski

Privileged members of North Korean society enjoy a meal at a restaurant. Military officers, top bureaucrats, party officials, diplomats, and business leaders receive many material benefits that ordinary citizens are denied.

lodge in the mountains near Wonsan in winter. They use foreign currency to shop at well-stocked government stores featuring a wide variety of foods and household goods. They also eat rich cuisine at the latest restaurants in the capital. As long as the parents do nothing to upset Kim or arouse suspicions of disloyalty, these families will thrive in the midst of a struggling nation. As Australian journalist Michael Pembroke noted after a recent visit, "There is a dark side of course, one that we could not see but which is well known. The repressive regime will not hesitate to eliminate opponents and can be guaranteed to allow the rural population to suffer before the elite class feels the effect of tighter sanctions."[17] Whether such a volatile system can survive in the modern world will be a crucial issue in years to come.

"The repressive regime will not hesitate to eliminate opponents and can be guaranteed to allow the rural population to suffer before the elite class feels the effect of tighter sanctions."[17]

—Michael Pembroke, Australian journalist

# CHAPTER THREE

## School Life

Attending school in North Korea, Ellie Cha worked hard at the usual subjects: reading, math, science, and history. It was only after she and her family defected to South Korea that she discovered her history lessons had mostly been wrong. For example, she was taught that South Korea and the United States had invaded North Korea to start the Korean War. That is the opposite of what actually took place. The North's version played up the leadership's glorious role in defending the nation. Cha also had to write essays before class in praise of heroes in the news. One essay described a man who had died trying to retrieve a portrait of Kim Il Sung from a burning building. She could not understand how a person could sacrifice himself for a dead leader. And not even the leader himself, but his portrait. "All of the education was focused on making loyalty for the government,"[18] Cha recalls.

### Indoctrination as the Main Goal

As Cha came to realize, the main purpose of the North Korean school system is not to educate young people but to indoctrinate (or condition) them to be loyal citizens. Beginning in kindergarten, children absorb the state ideology. This is juche, or national self-reliance, although Communist ideas still play a large part. The North Korean constitution states, "Through socialist education, for the sake of future generations and citizens, North Korea shall fight a revolution to raise its citizens with knowledge and virtue."[19] A child learns that everything is owed to the great men who came from Mount Paektu. She or he is drilled to memorize their exact titles: comrade Kim Il Sung, the Great Leader; comrade Kim Jong Il, the Great Guide; and the beloved and respected Kim Jong Un, the Supreme Commander. These names are to be spoken always with deep reverence.

At the same time, a child learns to be wary of North Korea's enemies. Japan, the United States, and South Korea all are viewed as evil and treacherous. "They are to be hated," says journalist Fyodor Tertitskiy, "so one should say not that 'an American died,' but rather 'an American scum kicked the bucket.'"[20] Children are taught that Kim Jong Un's nuclear program—what state media calls his "treasured sword"[21]—is necessary for the nation's survival. They are programmed to idolize Kim and his forebears as faultless leaders who rule with courage and wisdom. Like Cha, they learn a false version of history. In the state's version, Kim Il Sung and his armies laid waste to the Japanese and Americans with no help from China or the Soviet Union. No one is allowed to say that the Kim regime is a dictatorship.

> "I feel such pity for children in the system. They can't see the world but learn to live like that unconsciously."[22]
>
> —Yeon-ri Kim, who defected from North Korea

Students grow up accepting the regime as something that will always exist and cannot be changed. "I feel such pity for children in the system," says Yeon-ri Kim, who defected from North Korea. "They can't see the world but learn to live like that unconsciously."[22]

Students in North Korea face *kyoyang*, or indoctrination, all through their school years. As they proceed, the next most important thing is *kyoyuk*, or scientific knowledge and technical skill. The regime views *kyoyuk* as the key to the nation's economic advancement. These are the pillars that shape young North Koreans into loyal and useful citizens.

## Three Types of Schools

North Korea has three types of schools. The general school system is the main system that most students attend. It is free and compulsory for almost all North Korean children. The continuing education system is for adults seeking to learn new skills or tech-

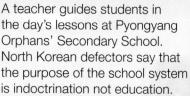

A teacher guides students in the day's lessons at Pyongyang Orphans' Secondary School. North Korean defectors say that the purpose of the school system is indoctrination not education.

niques. Special purpose schools are for talented young people and for children of the elite class.

In 2012 the Supreme People's Assembly changed the required number of years for students in the general school system from eleven to twelve. Under the new arrangement, students must attend one year of kindergarten, five years of elementary school, three years of middle school, and three years of high school. After high school, favored students can continue their education at a college or university. North Korea takes great pride in its school system and claims a literacy rate of 100 percent for children aged fifteen and older. Those who have fled the regime believe the actual percentage is much lower.

## Special Purpose Schools

Children who show signs of being intellectually gifted or having special talents are put into special purpose schools as young as age five. The regime tries to identify and support those who are

## Respect for Authority in a North Korean School

Monique Macias went to a military boarding school in North Korea. She and her family were guests of Kim Il Sung, who had befriended Macias's father, the former president of Equatorial Guinea. Macias found that strict student discipline was based in the Korean culture. As she recalls:

> At school I had always been curious to learn more, to ask questions, but it's very taboo in North Korea to question the teacher, and you certainly would not challenge the ideology or the history. But there seemed to be so many contradictions between what we were taught and what was true: there was supposed to be equality, but the differences between someone who was privileged, with family who worked in the party, and those [who did] not was obvious. But I always felt anxious and nervous asking questions that were too critical, and the teachers wouldn't go further.
>
> So why did me and the other students believe all [we were] taught? A lot of it is the influence of Korean culture. Korean culture is based around obeying those older than you. . . . You don't interrupt the father figure, and your opinion is second to his. Teachers are treated with the same reverence, what they say is how it is. . . . Questioning the teacher is completely unheard of. . . . It's as simple as that. There's no room for debate or questioning things—if you don't just repeat the lessons you'll fail. It's a collectivist society, not individualistic, and if you're different from the majority you'll be treated like a stranger.

Monique Macias, "What I Learned from a North Korean Education," *NK News*, March 14, 2014. www.nknews.org.

most likely to develop into great assets for the future. Being chosen for a special purpose school is a great honor. Many elite families resort to bribery of public officials to get their children accepted despite inadequate grades or no special signs of potential.

Special purpose programs last ten years. There are separate schools for the arts, sciences, foreign languages, and sports. Students undergo an intensive schedule, learning the value of hard work and discipline from the finest instructors. Schools that focus on physics, engineering, or computer technology produce graduates that are especially prized by the government. For example, Kim Jong Un's ambitious nuclear program is made possible by scientists who attended special purpose schools.

## Political Education in Elementary School

Children enter the general school system at age five, when they enroll in upper-level kindergarten. Some families send their children to lower-level kindergarten at age four. However, this lower-level year is not required. Some kindergartens are daytime only, while others board children overnight from Monday to Friday. In kindergarten, children learn music, dance, recitation, and drawing. They are taught to recognize a variety of animals. Like children everywhere, they love to work puzzles and play games together on the playground. They also begin their political education in earnest. Some kindergartens have an entire room devoted to Kim Il Sung and his descendants. These rooms contain portraits of Kim, a diorama of Kim's military outpost on Mount Paektu, and posters of the Kims' log cabin. Every school activity is linked to the nation's leaders. "The milk would arrive and we would go up one by one to fill our cups," recalls Lee Hyun-ji, who defected from the North. "The teachers would say: 'Do you know where the milk came from? It came from the Dear Leader. Because of his love and consideration, we are drinking milk today.'"[23]

> "The milk would arrive and we would go up one by one to fill our cups. The teachers would say: 'Do you know where the milk came from? It came from the Dear Leader. Because of his love and consideration, we are drinking milk today.'"[23]
>
> —Lee Hyun-ji, who went to elementary school in North Korea

Elementary school—or people's school, as it is called—begins at age six. Subjects include the Korean language, math, natural science, music, computer skills, and physical education. Many pupils also study English beginning in the third grade. Most important are the lessons in political thought. Children learn about juche and Socialist ethics in first and second grade. They are taught the supreme importance of the collective—that the collective good always outweighs the individual's needs and desires. Students attend classes such as "The Childhood of Our Great Leader Kim Il Sung" and "The Childhood of Dear Leader Kim Jong Un." Students also learn about Kim Jong Un's grandmother and her struggles against the Japanese. Lessons about the Kims consume almost seven hundred hours during the five years of elementary school. Students spend almost as much time learning about Kim Jong Un as they do studying the Korean language or math.

Discipline in elementary school is strict. Pupils sit rigidly and do not speak unless the teacher calls on them. Teachers stress obedience and tradition instead of creativity. Lessons focus on memorization and rote learning, with few chances for critical thinking. During the long school day, eating lunch and playing outside are the only occasions for students to socialize with friends.

Students look forward to special days to break the monotony. At age nine, each student joins the Korean Children's Union and swears allegiance to the state. Membership includes wearing a bright red neckerchief like the ones worn in the Young Pioneers, a youth group in other Communist states like China and Cuba. Songbun determines the order in which children are accepted into the organization. Students from elite families go first, followed by children of ordinary workers. Students whose parents are considered loyalty risks are still allowed to join, but they are last to receive the honor. Each year on Korean Children's Union Day, parents visit the elementary school to watch their children run an obstacle course and take part in mock military battles with grenades and Kalashnikov rifles made of plastic. In an interview with Singapore's *Straits Times*, Myong Hyon Jong, a ten-year-old who excels at math, says she wants to join the army to "safeguard the respected Supreme Leader Kim Jong-un with military power." She adds, "We have to prepare ourselves to defend our country."[24]

North Korea has poured funds into the development and training of promising young athletes such as these students at Pyongyang International Football (soccer) School. Gaining prominence on the global sports stage is one of Kim Jong Un's goals.

## Technical Skills in Secondary School

Secondary school, which includes middle school and high school, continues to educate students about their nation and beloved leaders. Classes begin at seven o'clock in the morning and continue until evening. Science and technical skills are stressed for their value to the nation. Students are encouraged to become computer scientists, engineers, biologists, physicists, and technicians to help North Korea advance in the world. Teaching methods concentrate on drill and repetition. Besides science, math, history, and the Korean language, the curriculum adds classes in English or some other foreign language, information technology, chemistry, biology, psychology, logic, and government policy. History lessons in secondary school are more sophisticated than the elementary ones but just as inaccurate. The main objective is still to shape citizens who obey the commands of the state with unswerving loyalty. A course in Chinese characters helps train students to conduct commerce with North Korea's neighbor. Students also take up military strategy and physical education classes to prepare them for military service, which is compulsory for both males and females.

Teachers assign mountains of homework in secondary school, ensuring that students have little free time outside the classroom. Weekends are spent in a generally hopeless attempt to catch up. Students are forced to adopt a disciplined schedule in order to succeed.

## Social Status and Higher Education

Following secondary school, students with the right social status are recommended for college. They seek to attend one of the nation's three main universities. Kim Il Sung University and Kim Chaek Technical University are located in Pyongyang, while Sungkyunkwan University is in Kaesong, a city in the North Hwanghae Province. Students chosen for these schools come from the most desirable social class, and they and their families have shown unwavering allegiance to Kim Jong Un, the party, and the ideals of juche. To get into Kim Il Sung University, students must have good grades in addition to family connections. Going to this prestigious school is a large step toward joining the ranks of the North Korean government elite.

"Even if your grades are better than anybody else among your peers, if you come from a lower-class family you cannot study at Kim Il Sung University."[25]

—Kim Yoo-sung, a blogger at the NK News website

However, not even academic excellence is enough for those with poor songbun status. "Even if your grades are better than anybody else among your peers, if you come from a lower-class family you cannot study at Kim Il Sung University," says Kim Yoo-sung, a blogger at the NK News website. "I came from a lower-class family in North Korea. Hence, students like myself wouldn't have been able to enter Kim Il Sung University no matter how excellent our grades were."[25]

Every year the Ministry of Education allots the number of students who can travel to Pyongyang and take the entrance exam

## Schools for Hackers

One notable area of success in North Korea's education system is computer science—or to be more exact, computer hacking. Experts worldwide note Pyongyang's surprising originality in coding methods. An army of well-trained computer whizzes have mounted cyberattacks on central banks and businesses in many different countries. Their most famous attack targeted a Hollywood studio. In 2014 Sony Pictures released *The Interview*, a comedy film that presented Kim Jong Un as a ridiculous tyrant. Shortly after the film's release, North Korean hackers calling themselves Guardians of Peace broke into Sony's computer system and stole thousands of documents. The hackers then posted online some sensitive personal data of Sony employees, including Social Security numbers, e-mail addresses, and executive salaries. They also published embarrassing details about actors under contract to Sony.

To create this army of hackers, the regime uses its school system. Students who show promise are tabbed as young as age eleven. They are sent to special schools, where they learn the latest hacking techniques and how to create computer viruses. According to a defector who knows about the regime's cyber training, the students are given a number of privileges. "Once you have been selected to get into the cyber unit, you receive a title that makes you a special citizen," he says, "and you don't have to worry about food and the basic necessities." Experts warn that if these hackers continue to improve, computers and smartphones the world over may be in serious danger.

Quoted in Timothy W. Martin, "How North Korea's Hackers Became Dangerously Good," *Wall Street Journal*, April 19, 2018. www.wsj.com.

for Kim Il Sung University or one of the other colleges. For example, the ministry might decide that four students from the city of Kimchaek can sit for the exam. A local committee at Kimchaek then selects four young people with good grades and sufficiently high social status to receive this opportunity.

Once enrolled at a university, students are supposed to get everything for free. However, as Kim Yoo-sung recalls, this is far from the case. "For instance, when your professor's child gets married, you have to pay some amount of money as a way of congratulating them on their marriage," he says. "There're so many other ridiculous things you have to pay for during your four years of college in North Korea. I had to pay for something required at college at least once every day."[26] He says many students would prefer to pay a flat tuition fee.

## Developing Skilled and Loyal Citizens

North Korea's government urges adults to better themselves in work-study programs. The nation's continuing education system enables adults to gain needed work skills. The system is connected to factories, farms, and fishing cooperatives. Everywhere from large cities to rural areas, workers can take classes at night or in monthlong intensive courses away from the workplace. This allows workers to learn new skills and techniques without losing their jobs. So-called farm colleges in the countryside teach engineering skills to agricultural workers. Some rural schools for adults offer basic subjects that laborers or peasant farmers never received as children. Workers also take correspondence courses or join together in evening study groups to improve their skills and knowledge. In some rural areas groups of five families combine into a team that is overseen by a local teacher or scholar. These five-family groups meet for study sessions every day after work. They also serve as surveillance teams for the government, reporting on suspicious behavior among other people in the area.

Although North Korea's school system is focused on conditioning young people to be loyal citizens, it also manages to produce scientists and technicians to compete in the modern world. One example is the rapid expansion of Kim Jong Un's nuclear program. Another is the proven ability of the nation's top computer experts to hack into foreign computer systems and bring them to a standstill. An education system that once seemed purely a propaganda tool has helped Kim become an even greater threat to his enemies.

# CHAPTER FOUR

## Work Life

The slogan in bright red characters hangs from a bus in the streets of a North Korean city: "Have you carried out the plan for today?"[27] It is one of hundreds of banners and posters on the walls of offices, train stops, restaurants, and gas stations. The slogans are part of a two-hundred-day speed campaign urging North Korean citizens to work harder and be more productive. Such campaigns are launched once or twice each year. The campaigns seek to overcome the effects of international sanctions, which are aimed at punishing the regime for its nuclear program and military threats to South Korea and other nations. The sanctions limit trade and hamper growth. Kim Jong Un tells his people that hard work will revive the economy. In this collectivist society, slackers are not tolerated. "If you look out the window, you won't see anyone just walking around," says Chang Sun Ho, who manages a small shoe factory in Wonsan, a port city on North Korea's east coast. "Everyone is working."[28] In fact, North Koreans consider it their patriotic duty to work.

### Working Life and the Party

North Korea contains a large population of workers. Approximately 59 percent of the people have regular jobs. Like so much else in North Korea, a person's working life depends on his or her relationship to the ruling party. The most desirable place to live and work is the capital city of Pyongyang. Working there is considered a great privilege and a sign of songbun status. Party members and those with ties to government officials are able to get jobs in the bureaucracy in Pyongyang. These jobs include many benefits not available to ordinary citizens. Upper-level personnel—officials, bureaucrats, scientists, and diplomats—drive cars, eat at fine restaurants, shop at well-stocked stores, and attend movies and musical performances. The party also assigns jobs to graduates from Kim Il Sung University or one of the other colleges. The best jobs go to graduates from high-status families under songbun. Those of medium status, even gifted students and hard workers, must settle for jobs in the middle and lower levels of the bureaucracy.

Another favored area of employment is businesses that earn foreign currency. Most operate in tandem with the party, the military, or powerful government agencies. The pay is not only better than at most other organizations but also more consistent. Competition for these jobs among children of high-status families can be fierce. Factories that Kim Jong Un visits and takes under his wing as examples of Socialist progress are especially generous to their workers.

North Koreans also covet jobs in the military. All males must serve in the military, most for a term of ten years. Since 2015 military service has also been mandatory for women, who must serve until age twenty-three. Most young people enlist after high school. Students who go on to obtain bachelor's degrees are required to serve only five years, and promising scientists or engineers only three. Young people must come from high-status families to qualify for top career positions in the military. Those who become lifelong officers, soldiers, and support staff are stationed in and around Pyongyang. They enjoy many privileges by way of the party. Their standard of living tends to be higher than that of nonmilitary citizens.

After ten years of military service, most discharged soldiers return home to work in local factories or farms. Less fortunate veterans are commandeered for other purposes. Each year the government sends thousands of veterans to work on large-scale building projects or to help favored businesses that need laborers. Former soldiers may find themselves toiling to erect a dam, a museum, or one more enormous monument to the Kims. These veterans have no choice but to obey.

## Little Choice of Jobs

Overall, people in North Korea have little choice in their occupations. Once the government assigns a person a job, it becomes that person's job for life. This is part of the Socialist system, in which the government decides how many workers are needed in each industry and assigns them accordingly. As a result, young people spend little time dreaming about becoming a doctor or a writer. They know from the start the decision is out of their hands. As Mina Yoon, who grew up in North Korea, explains:

> In reality, most kids in North Korea cannot even think about their future. They really don't have to, because the government makes choices on their behalf. Parents also do not bother worrying about their children's future because they

already know that what they want for their children will not make any difference. Upon graduation from high school, students fill out a form listing their top three career choices, but everyone knows it is nothing more than a formality. The government assigns the graduates with any jobs they think proper or necessary, and what the students want is not at all taken into account.[29]

Many graduates are given factory jobs simply because they live close to the factories. Once in place, they know their chance of getting a transfer is slight. Quite often these young workers do not want to move, since any new job would feature the same type of work for a similar salary and rations.

With opportunities so limited, some families are turning to bribery to obtain better jobs for their children. Yoon explains:

"Most kids in North Korea cannot even think about their future. . . . The government assigns the graduates with any jobs they think proper or necessary, and what the students want is not at all taken into account."[29]

—Mina Yoon, a defector who grew up in North Korea

There are certain steps to follow to get the desired job: first, you have to bribe the officers and steal your personnel record from the local administrative agencies. Then you have to bribe the factory managers or party secretaries so that they will issue letters of confirmation that they would like to hire you. Lastly, you have to submit the letter to the administrative agency in charge of assigning jobs. Everyone involved knows about the other parties' bribery, but they choose to overlook.[30]

Certain families regard bribery as a necessary expense. Determined parents begin saving money for this purpose while their son or daughter is still in secondary school.

# A Typical Workday in the Capital

Those lucky enough to get jobs in Pyongyang begin the workday early in the morning. At 6:00 a.m. the city awakens to the sound of patriotic music blaring from speakers attached to government vans. In thousands of apartments, office workers are getting dressed and bolting their breakfasts. Those living in upper-floor apartments have to leave for work a bit earlier to account for time taking the stairs. Before going out the door, workers always check to see that their special red lapel badges are pinned to their shirts or blouses. These badges feature the images of Kim Il Sung and Kim Jong Un. First introduced in the 1960s to demonstrate the loyalty of party members, the badges are now prized items on the

## Meeting Production Goals at a Shoe Factory

Like other businesses in North Korea, the small shoe factory in the port city of Wonsan is under pressure to meet government production quotas. Failure to do so would be unpatriotic. Chang Sun Ho, who manages the factory, says he and his 220 workers use locally made machines and domestic materials to produce nearly seven hundred pairs of shoes each day. Annual production goals are met in only six months. This example of North Korean self-reliance has drawn the attention of the nation's leader, Kim Jong Un. "The marshal [Kim] has said he has adopted this factory as if it were his own," says Chang. "So it is like we are working for our father. That's all the motivation we need."

Workers at Chang's factory do not need offers of bonuses or threats of being fired to motivate them. Most of their incentives come from peer pressure. Workers are organized in groups, and each group's output is displayed in large bar graphs on the factory walls for all to see. A drop in the group's production could lead to a worker being tagged as lazy. The work group is like a family, and no one wants to let down his or her family. "Normally, I work eight hours a day," says Kang Jong Jin, a former soldier employed at the Wonsan factory. "Now I sometimes stay longer. No one has to tell me to do it. I just do."

Associated Press, "Work Harder, North Korea Orders Citizens. But Does It Help?," June 23, 2016. www.ap.org.

black market. Elaborate ones can bring a few thousand won, the North Korean currency, or useful amounts of foreign money.

For a city of 3 million, there is surprisingly little traffic on the wide streets of Pyongyang. Commuters from outside the city ride to work on the crowded metros, or subway trains. Cars, trucks, and buses are specialty items, so many workers walk to the office or resort to bicycles. Some ride the locally built Sea Gulls, while others get secondhand imports from Japan. Either one requires several months' savings.

Regardless of how they get to the office, most workers arrive at their desks by seven thirty. Before work begins, they may read for a half hour or perform exercises. Reading includes office announcements, instructions for the day, or editorials in the party newspapers. The latter extol Kim Jong Un's latest exploits and shape the way citizens are to think about current events. At eight

Workers prepare kimchi (a traditional Korean dish made of fermented cabbage, cucumbers, and fiery red chilies) on a factory production line. Koreans who live near factories are often assigned factory jobs once they complete school.

## Forced Labor in China and Russia

One way Kim Jong Un's regime raises funds is by sending workers to China and Russia virtually as slave labor. About twenty-five thousand North Koreans work in the timber industry in eastern Siberia and on construction sites in western Russia. More than fifty thousand work in Chinese factories, construction sites, and restaurants. Thousands more are sent to countries in the Middle East and Africa. Exporting laborers brings North Korea about $2 billion to $3 billion a year, experts say. Of the $300 to $400 they earn each month, they get to keep only about 10 percent to 20 percent. The balance goes to the North Korean government agencies that arrange for the labor exports. Workers have no control over their contracts and cannot leave until a contract is finished.

Labor conditions for these workers are harsh. Often they work sixty to eighty hours a week. They are housed in tiny apartments with six to eight in a room. Nonetheless, many lower-status North Koreans are eager to obtain these foreign jobs. Some even bribe officials to get chosen. According to foreign affairs expert Joseph V. Micallef, "As brutal as it appears, for some, sadly, it is in fact a better quality of life than what is found in North Korea. Most workers acknowledge that they are better fed and have better medical care than their countrymen."

Joseph V. Micallef, "How North Korea Uses Slave Labor Exports to Circumvent Sanctions," Military.com, July 10, 2017. www.military.com.

office work commences. Although more offices are acquiring personal computers and copiers, much work is done by hand as it has been for decades.

Offices and factories provide an hour for lunch. Lunchtime in Pyongyang does not see a flood of workers on the streets and sidewalks as in other major cities. Most workers bring their lunch or, if they live nearby, hurry home to eat. Larger businesses offer a canteen on site with simple fare such as corn soup and corn cakes.

The workday generally ends at 5:00 p.m. However, most workers have to remain to take part in a so-called Community Session and Learning Session. In the Community Session, workers evaluate progress in the office or factory and prepare for the next day's work. The Learning Session combines lessons in political propaganda with rounds of criticism. Workers review their own job performance and also criticize colleagues for everything from being late to work to wasting office supplies. This routine is repeated each day of the working week, from Monday to Saturday.

To spur productivity, the regime occasionally decrees short-term periods of nonstop labor. In 2016 the government demanded seventy straight days of work with no days off. The state media called it the Battle of Seventy Days. During this furious ten-week period, harried workers were offered the chance to buy a vacation day if they wished. According to an anonymous source in Yanggang Province, "If you pay three Chinese yuan or half a U.S. dollar, you can officially take one day off."[31] However, the price was high: twice what many North Koreans earn in a month.

## Women and the Gray Markets

Women play a growing role in the workforce. Ninety percent of workers in factories and light industry are women, and they also hold a large number of white-collar office jobs. It is common for a woman to be the main wage earner in the household. This is in addition to cooking, cleaning the apartment, and caring for the children. The influx of women in the workforce has led to new rules. Female workers in Pyongyang are allowed to dress in bright colors and patterns and wear light makeup to the office. For some the makeup serves to hide skin blotches due to a poor diet. Long hair is permitted but must be securely tied back in an office setting.

Many women bring in extra money by trading items on the so-called gray markets. These markets, known as *jangmadang* in Korean, help ease some of the financial pressures of ordinary families. Hundreds of these marketplaces operate with tacit government approval across the nation. They accept Korean, Chinese, and American currency. With husbands stuck in state jobs with little pay and no future, many women thrive as traders in the informal markets. The gray markets began in the 1990s, when a deadly famine led women to sell mushrooms and scrap copper cable to help their families survive. A defector named Jung, who sends money to North Korea to support her mother's gray market trade in pigs and corn alcohol, says women are vital to the nation's econ-

omy. As Jung observes, "We North Koreans say men are fighting on the socialism front but women are fighting in the battle of life."[32]

## Working on Collective Farms

The battle of life can be particularly hard in the countryside. A large part of North Korea's population lives and works in rural areas, especially in the flatlands of the Northeast. Census statistics show that 40 percent of the population is rural, with 37 percent working in agriculture. More than 20 percent of the nation's gross domestic product comes from farming and fishing.

Workers harvest apples at a farm on the outskirts of Pyongyang. Rural residents who work on collective farms generally work long days, receive low pay, and must make do with simple tools and equipment for planting and harvesting.

Rural residents work in small factories or on collective farms. Those who work on farms ride their bikes on dirt roads to reach the fields early in the morning. Work teams mostly use simple tools in fields that are sloppily plowed. Instead of tractors and other types of farm machinery, they must rely on an ox. Workers learn to accept their lot of backbreaking labor for long hours. They earn the equivalent of one or two dollars a month. They also get ration coupons for food, but since the distribution system is all but broken for lack of resources, these are almost worthless.

For years every detail of farmwork, from which crops to plant to the targeted size of harvests, was tightly controlled by the government. Yet with floods, droughts, and botched attempts at central planning, the government has failed repeatedly to feed the nation. In 2016, for example, North Korea imported 300,000 tons (272,155 metric tons) of grain and still faced a deficit of almost 400,000 tons (362,874 metric tons) to reach the necessary supply.

## Small Signs of Reform

Under Kim Jong Un, the regime has introduced small reforms to improve crop yields. Families are allowed to work separately from the collective to grow fruits and vegetables on personal plots. They can then keep 30 percent of the proceeds. Should these families exceed production goals, they can sell the surplus to the state. However, many farmers are turning to the informal markets, where they can sell their produce for more money. "'Reform' remains a taboo word in the North," according to the *Economist* magazine. "But new measures in the countryside appear to [support] people farming for the market rather than for the state. It represents a tacit abandonment of state collectives in favor of family farming, and seems already to have had an effect."[33] Even small signs of the government easing its grip on people's working life are welcome to beleaguered North Koreans.

# CHAPTER FIVE

## Social Life

In the totalitarian regime of North Korea, not even family ceremonies are free from government meddling. In May 2016 Kim Jong Un suddenly canceled all weddings and funerals and banned movement in and out of the capital. The government was preparing for a major party congress and sought to avoid all possible mishaps. Once the congress was over, ceremonies could resume. At traditional weddings, guests watched the bride and groom place flowers beside a statue of Kim Il Sung, the Great Leader. The regime's disruption of social life and family observances was accepted with a shrug by loyal North Koreans.

### The Usual Pursuits of Teenagers

Authorities in North Korea preach moral uprightness and revolutionary discipline to the young. In this atmosphere a teenager's life in North Korea might seem cramped and drab. Yet young people in North Korean cities and villages manage to have fun in ways familiar to teens everywhere.

At night, while their parents bundle up in cold apartments, teenagers look for something to do. Households with a television might watch the state's limited menu of channels. More daring families view smuggled DVDs, especially action movies with Bruce Lee or Jackie Chan, over and over. Watching films from the United States or South Korea has its risks. Getting caught can earn a stretch in a labor camp or even worse. "You can be killed for watching American or South Korean films or dramas," says Ji-Min Kang, who grew up in North Korea before defecting. "You might say that's crazy, but if people understand freedom or know how people in other countries live, it is dangerous for the government."[34]

Bored teens sometimes escape to meet their friends on the street. They might wander into a video arcade, although the consoles tend to be slow and out of date. Pool halls and cafés are other popular hangouts. The main bowling alley in Pyongyang is expensive and accepts only American currency. On weekends kids with a little money go to bars. (The legal drinking age in North Korea is eighteen but is rarely enforced.) They drink ice-cold Taedonggang beer, which is brewed locally. Some sneak in bottles of Pyongyang Soju, a strong liquor, or Sufi, a Korean vodka. Young people know to be careful even while drinking with friends. If someone overhears a reckless remark criticizing Kim Jong Un or the regime, there could be trouble for the teens or their parents.

Occasionally, teenage friends will slip out to smoke cigarettes, made of either tobacco or hemp. Smoking is popular among males in North Korea—and legal for teens—but it is generally taboo for females. The sale and use of marijuana, however, is against the law. The hemp that is smoked in North Korea legally has much lower levels of THC—the ingredient responsible for a euphoric high—than marijuana. Drugs such as marijuana, opium, heroin, and crystal methamphetamine are widely available on the black market. As recently as 2005, government factories produced a potent form of crystal meth, which was then used to bring in cash through underground sales and from foreign buyers. Although the factories now are closed, meth chemists continue to pursue their trade in the shadows. Experts believe addiction rates are high in North Korean society—perhaps as high as 30 percent. Too often, teens facing a bleak future in Kim's police state turn to drugs as an escape.

A young couple enjoys a sunny day in a park at the foot of Mount Taesong. Although much of daily life is controlled by the government, young North Koreans still find ways to socialize and enjoy themselves when not in school or at work.

## Dating, Formal and Informal

The regime also exerts pressure on young people's romantic lives. Authorities promote conservative values based on Korean traditions. They urge young people to keep romantic feelings in perspective. "When it comes to relationships," says Kang, "Pyongyang tries to instill 'love for revolutionary comrades' over romance, but people reject it. When I lived in Pyongyang we couldn't travel around the country and didn't have any freedom of speech. But although the government succeeded in getting rid of these basic human rights, it couldn't prevent its people from falling in love."[35]

> "When it comes to relationships, Pyongyang tries to instill 'love for revolutionary comrades' over romance, but people reject it."[35]
>
> —Ji-Min Kang, who grew up in North Korea before defecting

## Crystal Meth as a Diet Drug

The party elite in North Korea lead lives far removed from the struggling mass of ordinary citizens. For example, recent reports suggest that wives of party officials are turning to crystal methamphetamine as a diet drug to lose weight. Experts say that meth use already has climbed to epidemic levels all over the country. Now it appears that male officials at the highest levels of the government obtain the drug from black market sources so their wives can use it to suppress their appetite. Why would elite officials go along with such a program? "They like their wives to be slim," says an unnamed source for the online news outlet *Daily NK*.

Addiction to meth has become a widespread national problem. Defectors claim that in some towns and villages nearly 80 percent of adults have tried the drug. What makes the story even more outrageous is the desperate need for food among the majority of North Koreans. As the *Daily NK* source said, "The average person has no time, let alone opportunity, to gain weight between mandatory work mobilizations and a shortage of food." The source suggests that the elite wives should lose weight by sending their surplus food to needy villagers.

Quoted in McCarton Ackerman, "Real Housewives of North Korea Taking Crystal Meth to Lose Weight," Fix, August 6, 2015. www.thefix.com.

Some families follow the old ways with their children. Teens are restricted to formal dates set up by agreement with other parents. Frequently, these are arranged with those of equally high status. A formal date might signal an interest in serious courtship. But increasingly, a more relaxed standard prevails. Young people go to dances at government-sponsored social clubs or take walks in the park. Mindful of the strides made by women in North Korean society, some teenage girls will ask a boy out on a date.

Often couples agree to meet at a movie theater or café. If parents forbid an evening date, a couple might meet on a weekend afternoon to roller-skate together on the city's large paved arcades or ride bikes in the park. (The regime frowns on females riding bicycles as a lewd activity, but it is still allowed.)

Gays and lesbians face even greater challenges. Homosexuality is such a taboo subject that there is no word for it in North Korea. With no sex education in schools, many gays do not understand their own feelings. Gays and lesbians tend to live alone or settle into a heterosexual marriage to avoid conflict with the state.

Old-fashioned moral ideas continue to hold sway. Couples walking together on the street never hold hands or show the slightest signs of public affection. It is not illegal, just not the cultural norm. The natural shyness of teenagers also contributes to this chaste practice. Kang recalls that he and his friends would keep their dates as secretive as possible:

> In my high school days when I was highly sentimental, my fellow students and I would go on dates in the park only when it was completely pitch black outside. High school students weren't allowed to freely date in the open. In this kind of environment, we had no choice but to see each other hidden behind the trees or in basements of apartment blocks late at night—or among others at group events like birthday parties.[36]

Considering their desire to remain out of sight, North Korean couples have two key advantages. There are few streetlights in cities and towns, and the electricity often does not work. For those seeking privacy, Pyongyang and other cities generally offer a welcome blanket of darkness at night.

## Delaying Marriage

Due to mandatory service, many young North Koreans delay getting married until they leave the military. On average, they do not marry until age twenty-seven. Males typically must serve ten years in the military after graduating from secondary school.

During their service they have little opportunity to meet women. This can lead to hasty decisions once they are out. As Kang explains:

> After military service a culture of introductions emerges for many men in their late 20s. Sometimes, relatives set these guys up with other people they know. And when North Koreans meet someone on [a] blind date, they have to take it seriously. So after military service, many men end up marrying the women their parents set them up with. This can mean that many North Korean husbands tend to be abrupt and not attentive at all.[37]

Males engage in premarital sex much more often than females, although that is beginning to change. The regime forbids sex education, bans all birth control, and promotes the idea of young women waiting until marriage to have sex. Kim Jong Un has urged women to get married and have children for patriotic reasons. His government even recruits young women to relocate to areas where a large number of bachelor soldiers are finishing their service. Kim wants couples to improve the nation's sagging birthrate and add to the number of future Socialist workers. Aside from government pressure, women have two major incentives to get married early. Women who are still single in their late twenties are considered spinsters, or old maids, in North Korean culture. In addition, women who marry between the ages of twenty-one and twenty-four are exempt from mandatory work. The government allows them to remain at home and care for their husbands and households instead of working long hours at a factory or office.

Most married couples choose to have children at once. Yet raising a child is expensive and time consuming. Despite Kim's urgent calls for couples to procreate, demand is high for illegal condoms smuggled in from China. It seems unlikely that the nation's birthrate will see a significant rise anytime soon.

## Weddings with Government Influence

Many marriages among children of the elite are still arranged the old-fashioned way, by the parents or by a hired matchmaker. More progressive families accept their children's decisions about whom to date and marry. Once marriage plans are made, the bride and groom soon learn that not even weddings are free from government intrusion. As the journalist Kim Yoo-sung notes, "In North Korea, your wedding isn't just *your* moment, because the government and Workers' Party often intervene. There's no such thing as a bouquet being thrown in the DPRK [North Korea], instead newlyweds bring flowers to pay respects to the statue of

On their wedding day, a North Korean couple poses for photographs at the Mansu Grand Monument. Newlyweds in Pyongyang are required by the state to bestow flowers at the foot of the monument to the country's two former leaders.

Supreme Leader Kim Il-sung immediately after their official ceremony."[38] And couples are forbidden to marry on April 15 and February 16. Those are the dates, respectively, of former leaders Kim Il Sung's and Kim Jong Il's birthdays.

Ordinary families hold weddings at the home of the bride's parents. Elite couples, however, might stage the ceremony at a fancy venue in Pyongyang, such as the glittering ballroom in the Koryo Hotel or a private room at the Okryu-Gwan restaurant.

## No Place for Religious Faith

Religious belief is all but outlawed in Kim Jong Un's North Korea. Believers from Buddhists to followers of the indigenous Ch'ondo religion must hide their true faith. Penalties are especially harsh for Christians. Although there are an estimated three hundred thousand to five hundred thousand Christians in the nation today, they have no freedom of worship. Pyongyang, which once held more Christians than any other city in the Korean Peninsula, is now entirely secular. Oddly enough, department stores there are allowed to display Christmas trees as a sign of the season, but any celebration linked to Christian beliefs can result in arrest, torture, or even public execution. No religion is allowed to take the place of Kim Jong Un's cult of power.

Open Doors, a watch group devoted to freedom of religion, ranks North Korea the world's worst offender of religious liberty. A 2017 report by the group Aid to the Church in Need estimates that between fifty thousand and seventy thousand Christians languish in North Korean prison camps. As a spokesperson for Open Doors explains:

Christianity is not only seen as "opium of the people" as is normal for all communist states; it is also seen as deeply Western and despicable. Christians try to hide their faith as far as possible to avoid arrest and being sent to a labor camp. Thus, being Christian has to be a well-protected secret, even within families, and most parents refrain from introducing their children to the Christian faith in order to make sure that nothing slips their tongue when they are asked.

Quoted in Doug Bandow, "North Korea's War on Christianity: The Globe's Number One Religious Persecutor," *Forbes*, October 31, 2016. www.forbes.com.

North Korean couples of every status reject modern wedding routines in favor of older customs. The bride wears the traditional *hanbok*, which is a flowing white dress embroidered with flowers. Some opt for more colorful *hanbok* of bright pink, red, and yellow.

Every North Korean wedding features a live hen and rooster wrapped in traditional cloths of vivid red and blue. As part of the tradition, guests file past to place flowers and dates into the hen's beak and red chili into the rooster's for good luck.

In atheist North Korea, the wedding itself includes no religious words or trappings. After the ceremony, guests toast the married couple and eat a variety of simple dishes. There sometimes are gifts, including small amounts of cash or household items. Nowadays couples often hire a wedding photographer to record the festivities on digital cameras or camcorders. And of course newlyweds in Pyongyang are required by the state to bestow flowers at the foot of the Kims' bronze statues at Mansu Grand Monument. Guests gather to capture the moment on their cell phones. Unless the couple is especially privileged, there is no honeymoon trip the next day. Husband and wife are expected at their jobs early in the morning without fail.

> "In North Korea, your wedding isn't just *your* moment, because the government and Workers' Party often intervene."[38]
>
> —Kim Yoo-sung, a journalist

## Holidays with a Political Angle

Workers under Kim's regime look forward to every two- or three-day break to celebrate a holiday. Besides New Year's Day, national holidays in North Korea are somber events marking milestones in the country's political history. Besides birthday celebrations for the Dear Leaders, including current leader Kim Jong Un, there is May Day (May 1) to celebrate International Workers' Day; Young Pioneers Day (June 6), which pays tribute to the regime's patriotic youth group; and the Workers' Party Day (October 10), which honors the beginning of the nation's ruling party.

The biggest public holiday of all is National Foundation Day on September 9. It marks the founding of the Democratic People's Republic of Korea and its liberation from Soviet control in 1948. Each year everything shuts down on this day. An enormous military parade, complete with bright red flags and banners, marching soldiers, tanks, artillery guns, and missiles on huge flatbed trucks, makes its way down the wide boulevards of Pyongyang as hordes of cheering onlookers clap their hands or pump their fists. "People would gather in the squares from morning until six o'clock and sometimes we would walk with the army," recalls Ji-Min Kang. "It was a very tiring intense day."[39] In the evening there are music and fireworks, and colorfully garbed couples gather to dance in the vast paved squares. Children are sure to get cookies and candy for one of the few times of the year.

## Little Time for Leisure

Those with means in Pyongyang and other outposts of the North Korean government enjoy various leisure activities. The capital city features a water park, an amusement park with rides, a concert hall, playing fields, golf courses, bowling alleys, and many other amenities. Yet the great majority of North Koreans have no time to think about leisure. Their days are filled with government-mandated work for little or no pay. Social life for these unfortunate citizens may amount to sipping a glass of tea with friends or relatives before trudging off to bed.

# CHAPTER SIX

## Political Life

On August 10, 2017, tens of thousands of North Koreans marched in Kim Il Sung Square in Pyongyang. The crowd was assembled on short notice to show support for the nation's leader, Kim Jong Un. President Donald Trump had publicly declared that the United States would meet North Korea's military threats with "fire and fury."[40] The mass of white-shirted citizens angrily raised their fists in the air, shouted slogans, and waved posters bearing patriotic messages. A crowd of elites in black shirts applauded the rallying workers as they filed past. The display of loyalty looked impressive when replayed on broadcasts in America and around the world. It appeared that the whole nation was ready to go to war. Yet defectors say such rallies are a sham, based mainly on people's fear of appearing disloyal.

### Making Political Use of Fear

Experts say that Kim's regime maintains power through the constant threat of violence. What might look like fanatical loyalty in Pyongyang's mass rallies, defectors say, is actually fear. The consequences of disloyalty—or even *appearing* to be disloyal—are prison camps and execution. One North Korean defector describes the cheering crowds as a show. "These civilians, if the government tells them to come, they are gathered by the system, they're forced to come, they don't have the freedom not to," he says. "People are scared. On the surface they look thankful, but none of it is genuine."[41] The defector himself refuses to give his name because his daughter still lives in North Korea. He fears what might happen to her should his remarks reach the ears of a government official. Thus, Kim's intimidation can extend far beyond his nation's borders.

Many observers question Kim Jong Un's sanity. At times he does seem mentally unstable, veering wildly from grand proclamations of unity and peace to threats of nuclear war. He spends one-fifth of the national budget on weapons while large numbers of his people starve. Yet at age thirty-four, this inexperienced dictator shows the same ability to keep his foes off balance that his father and grandfather had. Kim uses fear to his advantage even better than they did. It is the way he keeps his regime from collapsing, despite international sanctions, a failing economy, and a desperate people. According to foreign correspondent Cemal L. Ozgur, Kim is more cunning than his erratic behavior might suggest:

> The scenario is akin to a madman with a loaded gun who screams and fires shots into the air threatening to cause mayhem if his demands are not met. . . . No country wants to take any chances with the North because of the consequences, a missile or nuclear strike into a major metropolitan area is not worth any possible reward. Little do they know that underneath the mask lies a clever criminal that uses hysteria and fear to get people to do his bidding.[42]

Fear also works for Kim in keeping his top officials in line. Diplomats who depart for other countries must leave behind a son or daughter as hostage. Should the diplomat try to defect to the new country, the child's life would be forfeit. Since rising to power in 2011, Kim has ordered the executions of about seventy highly ranked aides. One of these was his own uncle—a shocking act to Koreans, who hold family ties to be sacred. One of Kim's advisors reportedly was executed for showing disrespect to the supreme leader. His crime: falling asleep in a meeting with Kim. Stories about such ruthless acts contribute to the people's persistent sense of dread.

North Koreans are always careful to show absolute loyalty to their country's leader, Kim Jong Un (center). A verbal confrontation with US president Donald Trump in 2017 brought tens of thousands of North Koreans out to march in support of their leader.

## The Appearance of Elections

North Koreans have no voice in their government's activities. Although elections are hailed as both a privilege and duty for patriots, voting is a sham. Propaganda posters tell the real story: "Let's all vote in agreement!"[43] Every four or five years, voters in 687 districts select deputies to the Supreme People's Assembly, the national legislature. All candidates come from the ruling Workers' Party. Kim Jong Un himself runs for office, as a candidate from Mount Paektu. People also vote for local officials, such as governors, mayors, and assembly members. Often there is only one name on the ballot for each office.

Voting is mandatory for everyone over age seventeen. Voters must register one month in advance. Elections may be pointless politically, but they do serve as both a census and a way for officials to monitor the adult population. As defector Mina Yoon notes, "The government checks the list of voters and if your name is not on the list, they will investigate it. It is often during [an] election that the government finds out about defectors."[44] According to Yoon, at election time defectors who are living in China slip back in to North Korea to register and vote. This is done to prevent the government from harming the families of defectors as retaliation.

Age or illness is no excuse for not voting. Mobile ballot boxes are provided for the elderly or those in the hospital. In national elections, there is nothing to mark. Ballots are already labeled with a single candidate's name. A voter simply drops the paper

## An Outpouring of Grief—or Fear?

On December 19, 2011, North Korea's state news agency announced the death two days earlier of leader Kim Jong Il from a massive heart attack. News reports showed an extraordinary outpouring of grief among citizens of the repressive nation. Soldiers dropped to their knees in anguish, citizens took to the streets sobbing and wailing, while children broke down in tears. Throughout ten days of national mourning, and for some days thereafter, the people continued to display their sorrow at the Dear Leader's death. Many burst into tears as they gathered at Kim's bronze statue in Pyongyang to leave flowers and wreaths. Chinese reporters described women so overcome with emotion that they fainted and fell to the ground.

Many observers outside North Korea questioned whether these tears were genuine or actually the product of fear. They wondered how people could mourn the passing of a leader who had trampled on their rights, denied them any voice in government, allowed them to starve, and threatened them with violence for years. Experts acknowledged that some North Koreans, fed the state's relentless propaganda since birth, probably felt true grief at the loss of a leader they had come to see as almost superhuman. Yet without doubt most reacted as they thought they must to satisfy the regime's demand for loyalty. A month after Kim's death, thousands of North Koreans received a six-month sentence to labor camp for failing to join the organized gatherings for mourners.

North Korean voters cast their ballots in an election. Only one name usually appears on the ballot for each elective office.

ballot in the appropriate box. Failure to vote is considered a major crime. It results in the person being sent to political prison.

## A Bizarre Criminal Code

Labor camps and political prisons are one of Kim Jong Un's main tools for spreading fear among the populace. Not voting is one of a wide variety of crimes that can land a person in a prison camp. Other examples include crossing the border without permission, spreading rumors that lead to distrust of the state, holding a religious service or being caught with religious materials, failure to hang government-provided portraits of Kim Il Sung and Kim Jong Il in the home, and watching American-made movies or reading books published in America. The US-based Committee for Human Rights in North Korea points out that the nation's criminal code authorizes the secret police to imprison tens of thousands of innocent citizens for crimes that are not really crimes. According to a report by the committee, "The revised criminal code makes it abundantly clear that many of its provisions allow authorities to deprive North Korean citizens of their liberties for, essentially, political offenses."[45] For example, the coach of the national soccer team was sentenced to several months of hard labor for his team's poor performance in the 2016 World Cup competition. A girl spent three years in a labor camp for singing along to a South Korean song at a private party. And everyone knows that severe crimes, such as outright traitorous behavior, are punished by hanging or firing squad.

> "The revised criminal code makes it abundantly clear that many of its provisions allow authorities to deprive North Korean citizens of their liberties for, essentially, political offenses."[45]
>
> —The Committee for Human Rights in North Korea

## Life in a Prison Camp

United Nations officials estimate that more than two hundred thousand North Koreans are held in prison camps, or *kwan-li-so*. Once sentenced to a North Korean prison camp, a person's life is forever changed, not to mention the lives of his or her loved ones. Like Joseph Stalin in the Soviet Union's political purges, Kim often makes an entire family pay for the supposed crimes of one individual.

Defector Kang Cheol-hwan was held at one of the worst: the Yodok concentration camp, also called Camp 15. Secluded in mountains about 62 miles (100 km) from Pyongyang, Yodok is designated for enemies of the state. Kang's parents had been loyal bureaucrats under Kim Il Sung but fell out with his son, Kim Jong Il, when they disapproved of him taking power merely because of his family name. Although only a child, Kang was imprisoned at Yodok along with his parents. He was forced

## Delaying the Olympics Broadcast

North Korea made quite a splash at the 2018 Winter Olympics in South Korea. At the opening ceremonies, Kim Jong Un's sister, Kim Yo Jong, made a glamorous appearance in the reviewing stand. The North Korean team delighted the crowd by marching into the stadium together with the South Korean team. And members of the North Korean women's hockey team joined with the South's squad to create the first joint Korean sports team in decades. Yet North Koreans had to wait to see any of these events, if they got to see them at all.

Members of the regime did not let enthusiasm about the Olympics override their instinct for censorship. The international broadcast was delayed in North Korea, and much of it went unseen. Officials in Pyongyang did not want to risk having their citizens hear hostile comments about Kim or his repressive regime. "North Korea likes to have as much control as they can over what their people see," said Jean H. Lee, a global fellow with the Wilson Center. "They don't like the unpredictability of live broadcasts, except for events that are completely scripted, like military parades."

Quoted in Holly Ellyatt, "North Korea Is at the Olympics—but North Koreans Probably Won't Get to See Much of It," CNBC, February 19, 2018. www.cnbc.com.

to haul loads of heavy wood for long distances. When a prisoner was hanged, Kang and the other inmates were ordered to throw rocks at the corpse for days. Defying orders led to confinement in a tiny cell inside the prison camp. "Most never survived the experience as they were forced to sit for extended periods in cold muddy water," says Kang. "If they survived, their flesh was literally rotten."[46] Kang spent ten years at Yodok before being released.

In a nation of food shortages, it is hardly a surprise that political prisoners suffer from hunger and malnourishment. Female prisoners are repeatedly subjected to sexual assault. All prisoners are forced to work long hours until they almost drop from exhaustion. If they survive their term, they are nonetheless marked for life as enemies of the state. Authorities regard them with suspicion to the end of their days. However, just surviving the camps is no small feat. "These are intended as one-way trips," says Phil Robertson, deputy director of Human Rights Watch Asia, "since the entire family is viewed as politically irredeemable and therefore can be abused, starved and ultimately worked to death."[47]

## A Nation Under Strict Control

Another way Kim keeps North Koreans in his grip is through tight control of all media. The regime has had great success in obstructing news from the outside world. Kang Shin-sam, an expert on North Korean technology, says, "There is no country which monopolizes and controls successfully the internet and information as North Korea does."[48]

Some information control is as simple as deleting archives of old newspapers and magazines. The regime wiped away digital copies of thousands of articles from the past seventy years. This was apparently done to hide discrepancies in the Kims' version of history. For example, articles from the 1950s describe Kim Il Sung working with a small circle of colleagues to govern the nation. The regime's official story is that Kim Il Sung was the sole ruler from the start. Also deleted are more recent articles about Jang Song Thaek, Kim Jong Un's uncle and mentor, whom Kim executed as a supposed traitor. Jang has now been virtually erased from North Korean history.

Other forms of censorship call for the most up-to-date technology. Though smartphone use in the country is growing—and becoming something of a status symbol—most citizens are limited to a government-created intranet instead of the World Wide Web. This intranet is not connected to the external Internet and features only information approved by the government. The regime also uses smartphones and computers to spy on their users. Almost all smartphones, laptops, tablets, and computers in North Korea run on the Red Star operating system developed by Kim's engineers. Red Star guides users to certain sites on the intranet, such as Kim's speeches or national recipes. At the same time, it allows authorities to monitor the user in several ways. It can record the user's browsing history, delete files from the user's laptop, and block the user from sharing files. The regime also employs a more hands-on approach to blocking information. On the street, smartphone users must submit to random stops by the police, who check the content of their phones for illegal material.

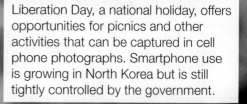

Liberation Day, a national holiday, offers opportunities for picnics and other activities that can be captured in cell phone photographs. Smartphone use is growing in North Korea but is still tightly controlled by the government.

Some hope that increased use of smartphones will help destabilize Kim Jong Un's regime. Even if information from the outside world is still limited, more of it is getting through. This might reduce the effectiveness of Kim's propaganda machine. In testimony before the US Congress, former North Korean diplomat Thae Yong Ho said, "The domestic system of control is weakening as the days go by."[49] Other experts disagree. They say allowing more smartphone use might actually strengthen the regime's control. After all, smartphones not only provide messaging and games but also a ready conduit for propaganda and a handy tool for surveillance. It remains to be seen whether North Korea can advance into the modern world while continuing to hold its citizens in a police state.

# SOURCE NOTES

## Introduction: The Hermit Kingdom

1. Quoted in Victor Mallet, "North Korean Defector Hyeonso Lee on Escape and the Secretive State," *Financial Times*, February 9, 2017. www.ft.com.
2. Quoted in Sean Illing, "Fear, Loneliness, and Duty—an American Journalist on Daily Life in North Korea," Vox, November 29, 2017. www.vox.com.
3. Quoted in Alexandra Ma, "Kim Jong Un Reportedly Laughed Off His 'Little Rocket Man' Nickname over Noodles and Wine with South Korea," Business Insider, March 9, 2018. www.businessinsider.com.
4. Quoted in Charlie Campbell, "Freedom, Sanctions and North Korean Ice Cream: Q&A with Defector Hyeonseo Lee," *Time*, May 27, 2016. www.time.com.

## Chapter One: A Nation Under Rigid Control

5. Quoted in Katy Galimberti, "Flooding Disaster in North Korea: How Rare Is It for the Country to Accept Outside Relief?," AccuWeather, September 26, 2016. www.accuweather.com.
6. Jordan Weissmann, "How Kim Jong II Starved North Korea," *Atlantic*, December 20, 2011. www.theatlantic.com.
7. Lucian W. Pye, "The North Korean Revolution, 1945–1950," *Foreign Affairs*, March/April 2003. www.foreignaffairs.com.
8. Quoted in Christopher Richardson, "North Korea's Kim Dynasty: The Making of a Personality Cult," *Guardian* (Manchester), February 16, 2015. www.theguardian.com.
9. Quoted in Antonia Blumberg, "How North Korea's Political Ideology Became a De-Facto Religion," *Huffington Post*, April 27, 2017. www.huffingtonpost.com.
10. BBC, "Profile: North Korean Leader Kim Jong-un," August 29, 2017. www.bbc.com.
11. Quoted in Alastair Gale, "North Korea's 'Military First' Policy Threatens to Blunt Impact of Sanctions," *Wall Street Journal*, March 3, 2016. www.wsj.com.

## Chapter Two: Family Life

12. Michael Turtle, "Life in North Korea," Time Travel Turtle. www
.timetravelturtle.com.
13. Quoted in Phil Robertson, "North Korea's Caste System,"
*Foreign Affairs*, June 30, 2016. www.foreignaffairs.com.
14. Je Son Lee, "Ask a North Korean: How Common Is Abortion
in North Korea?," *NK News*, July 6, 2017. www.nknews.org.
15. Julie Makinen, "At a North Korean Nursery School, Tots Get
an Early Education in Weaponry," *Los Angeles Times*, May 4,
2016. www.latimes.com.
16. World Food Programme, "Democratic People's Republic of
Korea," 2018. www1.wfp.org.
17. Michael Pembroke, "The Privileged Elite of North Korea Live
a Charmed Life," *Sydney Morning Herald*, May 2, 2017. www
.smh.com.

## Chapter Three: School Life

18. Quoted in Leslie Young, "Meet Ellie Cha, the North Korean
Defector Working on Parliament Hill," Global News, November 5, 2017. https://globalnews.ca.
19. Quoted in Ha-kyung Angela Kim, "Inside North Korea's Education System," Foreign Policy News, February 23, 2017.
http://foreignpolicynews.org.
20. Fyodor Tertitskiy, "Life in North Korea—the Early Years,"
*Guardian* (Manchester), December 21, 2015. www.theguard
ian.com.
21. Quoted in Jean H. Lee, "How North Korean Children Are
Taught to Hate Americans," *Newsweek*, July 6, 2017. www
.newsweek.com.
22. Quoted in Kim, "Inside North Korea's Education System."
23. Quoted in Anna Fifield, "North Korea Begins Brainwashing
Children in Cult of the Kims as Early as Kindergarten," *Washington Post*, January 16, 2017. www.washingtonpost.com.
24. "North Korean Students Throw Mock Grenades in Celebration of
Children's Day," *Straits Times* (Singapore), June 6, 2017. www
.straitstimes.com.
25. Kim Yoo-sung, "Family Background Is a Prerequisite, but Students Need the Grades Too," *NK News*, August 26, 2015.
www.nknews.org.

26. Kim, "Family Background Is a Prerequisite, but Students Need the Grades Too."

## Chapter Four: Work Life
27. Quoted in Associated Press, "Work Harder, North Korea Orders Citizens. But Does It Help?," June 23, 2016. www.ap.org.
28. Quoted in Associated Press, "Work Harder, North Korea Orders Citizens. But Does It Help?"
29. Mina Yoon, "Bribery and Birthright: How to Get a Job in North Korea," *Guardian* (Manchester), April 29, 2014. www.theguardian.com.
30. Yoon, "Bribery and Birthright."
31. Quoted in Rishi Iyengar, "North Koreans Can Either Work 70 Days Straight or Pay to Take a Day Off," *Time*, March 14, 2016. www.time.com.
32. Quoted in Ju-min Park, "In North Korea, Men Call the Shots, Women Make the Money," Reuters, May 24, 2015. www.reuters.com.
33. *Economist*, "Spring Release," February 26, 2015. www.economist.com.

## Chapter Five: Social Life
34. Quoted in Maya Oppenheim, "What It's like to Be a Teenager in North Korea," *Independent* (London), September 9, 2016. www.independent.co.uk.
35. Ji-Min Kang, "Dating, North Korean Style," *Guardian* (Manchester), April 22, 2014. www.theguardian.com.
36. Kang, "Dating, North Korean Style."
37. Kang, "Dating, North Korean Style."
38. Kim Yoo-sung, "Ask a North Korean: What Happens on Your Wedding Day?," *Guardian* (Manchester), August 3, 2015. www.theguardian.com.
39. Quoted in Oppenheim, "What It's like to Be a Teenager in North Korea."

## Chapter Six: Political Life
40. Quoted in *Independent* (London), "North Koreans Stage Massive Rally in Show of Defiance Against Donald Trump," August 10, 2017. www.independent.co.uk.

41. Quoted in Jimmy Nsubuga, "North Defector Reveals Why They Follow Kim Jong Un," *Metro* (London), August 14, 2017. https://metro.co.uk.

42. Cemal L. Ozgur, "Kim Jong-un Is Not Crazy," GlobePost, August 6, 2017. www.theglobepost.com.

43. Quoted in Danielle Wiener-Bronner, "Yes, There Are Elections in North Korea and Here's How They Work," *Atlantic*, March 6, 2014. www.theatlantic.com.

44. Quoted in Wiener-Bronner, "Yes, There Are Elections in North Korea and Here's How They Work."

45. Quoted in Harvey Gavin, "Three Years Hard Labour for SINGING—North Korea's Brutal Criminal Code Revealed," *Express*, November 17, 2017. www.express.co.uk.

46. Quoted in Lydia Smith, "Life Inside a North Korea Labour Camp: 'We Were Forced to Throw Rocks at a Man Being Hanged," *Independent* (London), September 28, 2017. www.independent.co.uk.

47. Quoted in Rebecca Pinnington, "Brutal Life of North Korea Children: Propaganda in Schools and Forced to Watch Executions," *Express*, November 4, 2017. www.express.co.uk.

48. Quoted in Timothy W. Martin and Warangkana Chomchuen, "North Koreans Get Smartphones, and the Regime Keeps Tabs," *Wall Street Journal*, December 6, 2017. www.wsj.com.

49. Quoted in Martin and Chomchuen, "North Koreans Get Smartphones, and the Regime Keeps Tabs." *Wall Street Journal*, December 6, 2017. www.wsj.com.

# FOR FURTHER RESEARCH

## Books

Barbara Demick, *Nothing to Envy: Ordinary Lives in North Korea*. New York: Spiegel & Grau, 2010.

Travis Jeppesen, *See You Again in Pyongyang: A Journey into Kim Jong Un's North Korea*. New York: Hachette, 2018.

Jang Jin-sung, *Dear Leader: My Escape from North Korea*. New York: Atria, 2014.

Hyeonseo Lee, *The Girl with Seven Names*. New York: William Collins, 2016.

Daniel Tudor and James Pearson, *North Korea Confidential: Private Markets, Fashion Trends, Prison Camps, Dissenters and Defectors*. North Clarendon, VT: Tuttle, 2015.

## Internet Sources

Nicole Crowder, "The Structured, Guarded World of North Korean Schools," *Washington Post*, October 12, 2015. www .washingtonpost.com/news/in-sight/wp/2015/10/12/the-struc tured-guarded-world-of-north-korean-schools/?utm_term=.44 85b924797c.

Fuchsia Dunlop, "Eating in North Korea: 'We Were Being Fed a Story,'" *Financial Times* (London), September 21, 2017. www .ft.com/content/1f9bbfc0-9d93-11e7-9a86-4d5a475ba4c5.

Felicity Harley, "Inside the Strange, Complicated Lives of North Korean Women," *New York Post*, August 28, 2017. https://ny post.com/2017/08/28/inside-the-strange-complicated-lives-of -north-korean-women.

Will Ripley, "Inside Pyongyang: How North Korea Is Changing," CNN, February 26, 2017. www.cnn.com/2017/02/26/asia/north -korea-will-ripley/index.html.

Melia Robinson, "A Photographer Captured These Dismal Photos of Life in North Korea on His Phone," Business Insider, Febru-

ary 15, 2018. www.businessinsider.com/photos-of-life-in-north
-korea-2017-8.

Jon B. Wolfsthal, "Kim Jong Un Makes America Irrelevant," *Atlantic*, March 7, 2018. www.theatlantic.com/international/archive
/2018/03/kim-jong-un-offers-to-hold-nuclear-talks/555002.


## Websites

**Democratic People's Republic of Korea** (http://korea-dpr
.com). This is the official web page of the North Korean regime. It
offers a mix of government propaganda and news about tourism
and business in the Socialist state.

**Liberty in North Korea** (www.libertyinnorthkorea.org). This website covers the history of North Korea as well as the changes
occurring in its repressive society. This is a good source to learn
about many different aspects of the Hermit Kingdom.

*NK News* (www.nknews.org). This website features excellent articles and analyses of current events in North Korea. Writers cover
the latest political developments in Pyongyang while also providing in-depth looks at the lives of ordinary North Koreans.

# INDEX